POSSESSING THE GATE

OMOBOLA JEFFREYS

All rights reserved. No part of this publication may be reproduced, stored in a retrieval system, or transmitted in any form or by any means, electronic, mechanical, photocopying, recording, or otherwise without prior written permission of the publisher. The only exception is brief quotation in printed reviews. Most quotations are taken from the Holy Bible King James Version, unless otherwise stated.

Designed & Layout and Cover Image by: PhizleGraphics

FOREWORD

Every gate needs to be manned and everyone has the right to choose how the gates of their lives are possessed. This book introduces the reader to prayerful possession and manning of their gates it leads through important scriptural notations used as anchors for the reader.

Dr. Omobola Jeffreys introduces the reader through a series of gates that needs to be possessed, with clear directions on how these gates can be effectively possessed by their rightful owners.

As you read pray along, may you possess your gates and may they yield great increase in line with the word of God.

D Jeff.

2   POSSESSING THE GATE

CONTENTS

CHAPTER 1	Ease for a lifetime
CHAPTER 2	Ease of Passage
CHAPTER 3	Ease of Restoration
CHAPTER 4	Ease of Increase
CHAPTER 5	Ease of Appointment
CHAPTER 6	Ease of Supernatural Remembrance
CHAPTER 7	Ease of Marital Reward
CHAPTER 8	Ease of Possession
CHAPTER 9	Ease of Access
CHAPTER 10	Ease of Supernatural Help

INTRODUCTION

Many people go through life struggling as they go. However, for the few who choose to ask God for instruction and direction, the journey is easy. Just like when one visits a new place, having some allocated support will save one from distress . For those who realize this crucial truth later in life, their path tends towards difficulty and some crucial time may be lost.

For this reason, God has helped me to put together a few prayer points, with the scripture as a pivot. These prayer points will help you to pray aright as you possess all that God has in store for you.

CHAPTER 1:
EASE FOR A LIFETIME

1. Lord, thank you for leading me into a lifetime of ease as I enter this new season.

2. I walk into and take possession of the ease provided for every season and month of this year.

Psalm 25:13-15 (KJV)

His soul shall dwell at ease and his seed shall inherit the earth. 14 The secret of the Lord is with them that fear him and he will shew them his covenant. 15 Mine eyes are ever toward the Lord for he shall pluck my feet out of the net.

Ease leads to inheritance while difficulty leads to lack of results

3. The ease that makes results obvious shall be my testimony this season, through this month and through this year.

- *The body cannot function well when the soul is troubled. No matter your physical possession, attainment and condition, you cannot thrive when your soul is troubled.*

4. Lord, in this season, my soul shall dwell at ease my

soul shall not be under duress. *Your soul can be well only for a short while if your body is diseased.*

5. My body shall not be under any duress in this season, this month and for the rest of the year.

   Jeremiah 46:27b (ASV)

   Jacob shall return, and shall be quiet and at ease, and none shall make him afraid.

6. Every troublesome habitation that has held me captive in the years before now, today, I gain freedom from you and I decree ease on my return.

   - *When the prodigal son returned, he was anticipating difficulty, but the mercy of God eased his way back into his inheritance.*

7. Lord, it doesn't matter how far I have erred and journeyed away from my destiny, and the provisions made for me under grace, today, I receive a restoration with ease.

   Psalm 45:7 (KJV)

   Thou loveth righteousness and hated wickedness, therefore lord, thy god has anointed you, with the oil of gladness above your fellows.

- *Oil lubricates   what was laborious becomes easy once you receive the oil of gladness. This ushers in ease that makes you rejoice.*

8. Father, in this season, this month and year, I make an allegiance to you and I declare that righteousness will be my watch-word.

9. Father, as I embrace righteousness, I receive the oil of gladness.

- *Favour and approval bring ease. What has been difficult becomes easy when someone chooses to help you.*

10. Lord, in this new season, I receive the help and approval of they that will make my journey easy.

11. Lord, stir the heart of they that will bring me ease. Give them no rest until they have done that which you have allocated to them to do for me.

Isaiah 45: 1-3

Thus saith Jehovah to his anointed, to Cyrus, whose right hand I have holden, to subdue nations before him, and I will loose the loins of kings to open the doors before him, and the gates shall not be shut: 2 I will go before thee, and make the rough places smooth I will break in pieces the doors of brass, and cut in sunder the bars of iron 3 and I will give thee the treasures of darkness, and hidden riches of secret places, that thou mayest know that it is I, Jehovah

- *The lord has shown clearly here that He has held the hand of Cyrus and subdued the nations before Cyrus arrives. The results that Cyprus would get were not dependent on his sweats they were dependent on what God would achieve for him before he makes any effort.*

12. As you have done for Cyrus, lord, I know that you can do for me. For this reason, Lord, I ask that you win battles and victories for me before I arrive at the battle front in Jesus name.

13. According to your word, Father, subdue the nations before I arrive at my destinations in this season, through the months and the year.

    Loin stands for strength and stamina. When the loin is loose, the stamina has been compromised and the individual is feeble and no longer grounded. When

God looses the loins of kings, their territories are ready to be plundered.

14. Father, loose the loin of kings so no one will have the power to oppose the placements that you have allocated to me.

15. Lord, make the inhabitants of the lands of my possession open to be subdued.

16. Father open the doors of access I need and enforce that no door of favour is shut against me through this season, month and year.

17. Father, every brass door that has resisted and defeated me for years, as I re-access them in this season, month and year, they shall be broken into pieces in the name of Jesus.

18. Every iron gate that has been cast to prevent my progress, at my appointed time of arrival, in this season, month and year, father I authorize a heavenly thunder to break through and melt them in the name of Jesus.

• *Roughness causes abrasion, roughness causes*

distress, roughness causes wounds.

19. Father, go ahead of me and make every rough place smooth before I arrive.

20. All hidden riches that lie where I will tread in this season, month and year, Lord I ask that you give them into my possession.

Psalm 23:5

You prepare a feast for me in the presence of my enemies.

- *We all know that one of the ways the enemy tortures its victim is to deprive them of sustenance. When God chooses to give you ease, He takes away the power of the enemy to oppress. When someone is planning to make you hungry, but God sets up a feast of fat things – heyyyy!*

21. Lord, I welcome a feast of fat things that will silence the intentions of the oppressors in this season, this month and the rest of the year.

- *You honour me by anointing my head with oil, my cup overflows with blessings. When ease comes, it brings honour with it....suddenly, people are drawn to ask you how you do it - those who asked – "who are you?" will start saying "how are you".*

22. Lord, let your ease bring me honour throughout this season, month and year.

• *In some cases, the ease that will bring restoration is tied to our actions David had lost family and possessions. To get this back, he needed to go and fight. In the process of fighting, he could lose men...he needed information David was kind to a wounded man - thereafter, the man gave him all the information he needed to make his journey easier.*

23. Lord, the key to my ease is in my hands, help me to switch on my season.

• *Association can take stress out of your life.*

24. Lord, they that I need to meet and know, who are scheduled to lead me into easy green pastures, I welcome them into my life through this season, month and year.

When a tree is taller than the rest, there is no doubt it

will soak in more sun than the rest.

25. Lord, give me a preferred allocation that will distinguish me from the rest and enable me to get prompt result.

Congratulations on your prayers today I declare that all that you have struggled and laboured over before you achieved in previous years, from this season month and year will now come to you on a platform of ease.

14   POSSESSING THE GATE

CHAPTER 2:
EASE OF PASSAGE

No one can navigate easily through life except by supernatural help . The world answers to uniqueness. Only those who are different get singled out . For this reason , we need God to order our path through life

1 Samuel 3:1-3 (KJV)

And the child Samuel ministered unto the LORD before Eli. And the word of the LORD was precious in those days there was no open vision.[2] And it came to pass at that time, when Eli was laid down in his place, and his eyes began to wax dim, that he could not see [3] And ere the lamp of God went out in the temple of the LORD, where the ark of God was, and Samuel was laid down to sleep

- *Samuel heard God, when the voice of God was scarce, even the town's ordained prophet acknowledged this encounter. It is what I have that others don't have that will give me the ease and recognition I need.*

1. Lord, in this season, open my eyes to what you have put inside me that is unique that the world needs.

- *When the encounter was over, Eli didn't argue with Samuel, he knew that what he was saying was right . No one argues with results.*

2. Through my results in this season , give me a platform that will showcase my excellence to the world

- *Samuel was in Eli's house, a man who himself had heard God before. Despite that , it took a couple of walks for Samuel....to be told that it was God speaking.... Some so called superiors are the ones to hinder the greatness heading your way.*

3. Father, through this season, month and year, hand me over to destiny custodians who have what it takes to lead me to my throne..

4. Through this season, month and year, I separate myself from custodians who will jeopardize my opportunity for greatness through jealousy, anger and sheer wickedness

- *Serious mistakes make life difficult there are pitfalls that are costly and will always be a foothold for the enemy. Jacob stepped into one of those pitfalls.*

   A journey of 7 years turned to 14 years with hard labour and oppression. He had to fight hard to get what one should normally get with ease. He started well into what was meant to be a straight journey which later got twisted.

5. Lord, I secure myself from errors that will prolong my journey through life to greatness.

6. Lord, every pitfall that will exchange my ease for hardship, I ask that your mighty hand deliver me from such in Jesus name.

7. I receive the spirit of discernment to protect me from any carelessness, so I will not hand my destiny over to difficulties

- *Regarding Jacob, after a while, God decided it was enough. When his father in law wanted to add more stress, God stepped in - gave him wisdom to ease his way out. God taught him a trick to acquire more animals, therefore, more wealth.*

8. For the hardship I have led myself into, there is a way out...lord, from this season, month, year and onwards, show me the easy way out of my misery.

- *God didn't stop there   God then warned his father in law..."don't bother him".*

9. From today, lord, send a stern warning that cannot be

overlooked, to them who have promised to make life difficult for me.

Matthew 2:1-4, 7-8 MSG

After Jesus was born in Bethlehem village, Judah territory— this was during Herod's kingship—a band of scholars arrived in Jerusalem from the East. They asked around, "Where can we find and pay homage to the newborn King of the Jews? We observed a star in the eastern sky that signalled his birth. We're on pilgrimage to worship him." When word of their inquiry got to Herod, he was terrified—and not Herod alone, but most of Jerusalem as well. Herod lost no time. He gathered all the high priests and religion scholars in the city together and asked, "Where is the Messiah supposed to be born?" Herod then arranged a secret meeting with the scholars from the East. Pretending to be as devout as they were, he got them to tell him exactly when the birth-announcement star appeared. Then he told them the prophecy about Bethlehem, and said, "Go find this child. Leave no stone unturned. As soon as you find him, send word and I'll join you at once in your worship."

- *Not everybody who celebrates with you is happy with*

your success.

10. Lord, every pretending 'rejoicer', who comes with intent to harm, your word says that 'you frustrate the token of liars' I decree that heaven will frustrate their tokens in Jesus name.

- *Ease can come as free passage devoid of any difficulty or God shielding you from wounds during attack. God gave Joseph information that will prevent confrontation leading to destruction. I like to avoid confrontation if I can. God said to Joseph...take that child, run now. There is an ease of passage which makes you to pass over without fighting at all. Some like fighting and showing scars, some of us don't have to fight at all.*

11. Lord, give me regular updates that will save me from unnecessary battles that will scar me.

- *You wonder why Jesus Christ still makes impact centuries after his death nobody gets announced and remains hidden.*

- *Jesus' conception got announced*

    - *Mary was notified, Joseph too.*

- *Jesus' pregnancy got announced*

  \-   *Elizabeth felt a kick.*

- *Jesus' birth got announced*

  \-   *The wise men saw the stars and angel.*

- *Jesus' readiness got announced*

  \-   *Spirit like a dove.*

- *Jesus' death got announced*

  \-   *The temple curtains tore.*

- *Jesus' resurrection got announced*

  \-   *The angel at the tomb.*

- *Announcement is crucial for ease of passage*

  Life can be hard for someone who has no one who believes in them some people have what it takes they just need a little exposure. No matter what you are carrying, sometimes, you just need someone to say, 'I attest to it that he or she is good'. That is called reference.

LUKE 1:40-45 (GNT)

She went into Zechariah's house and greeted Elizabeth. When Elizabeth heard Mary's greeting, the baby moved within her. Elizabeth was filled with the Holy Spirit and said in a loud voice, "You are the most blessed of all women, and blessed is the child you will bear! Why should this great thing happen to me, that my Lord's mother comes to visit me? For as soon as I heard your greeting, the baby within me jumped with gladness. How happy you are to believe that the Lord's message to you will come true!

12. Lord, confirm me to people who are credible who will announce and affirm me.

13. Lord, align me with people who will ease my passage into worldwide recognition. Not for everyone

14. Lord, raise voices for me in the places that matter, in this season.

15. Lord, make men and women go out of their way to connect me to my outstanding results, in this season.

16. Father, earmark me for a peaceful passage this season, month and year.

a) No negative publicity.

b)   No negative labels.

c)   No victimization.

17.   Let no man trouble me this season, month and year through my ease of passage.

a)   Not from people on my level

b)   Not from people above me.

c)   Not from people below me.

d)   I will not be silenced by the wickedness of men.

18.   Every unrighteous persons and authority who chooses to make life unbearable for me, I decree, will find no rest or find peace until they stop.

- *Let no man trouble me, for I bear upon my body the marks of Christ.*

19.   Oppression will cease from my door now in Jesus name.

- *When a grown family man is crying for the fear of going out to work, because a man who was raised to torture another is now in a place of authority, then you know that there is a problem,*

20. Lord, every oppressor who will take away my peace and stop me from achieving greatness and excellence, I take power out of their hands, and I render them unable to achieve their plan.

- *Growing up in a farming family, I know the difference between weeding a land before planting and planting on a land that has been weeded and ready - results are sweat-less and you cover more grounds.*

21. Subdue nations before me because it's easy to gain speed when the hands of the wicked have been tied.

22. Send help ahead of me to clear my way and to remove hardship

- *There are humans who can sense greatness from afar and will stop at nothing to destroy it.*

23. Today, I permanently blindfold very evil eye that censors greatness with the purpose of causing termination.

24. Every eye that seeks out greatness but causes the greatness to fizzle out in broad daylight, receive blindness in Jesus name.

25. Every eye that looks for the purpose of evil monitoring, today, I take vision away from you, I declare a blindness that will never be cured.

- *When people are born, a path is set if everyone follows their designated path, no one is meant to waste, however, many don't.*

I decree

26. MY path in life shall not be diverted through difficulty

27. MY path in life shall not be swamped with wickedness.

28. MY journey will not be delayed by the hand of the enemy

29. I shall not experience difficulty or distress as I achieve purpose.

Congratulations on your prayers today I declare that all that you have struggled and laboured before you achieved in previous years, from this season month and year will now come to you on a platform of ease.

CHAPTER 3:
EASE OF RESTORATION

2 KINGS 8:1-6

Elisha had told the woman whose son he had brought back to life, "Take your family and move to some other place, for the Lord has called for a famine on Israel that will last for seven years." 2 So the woman did as the man of God instructed. She took her family and settled in the land of the Philistines for seven years.3 After the famine ended she returned from the land of the Philistines, and she went to see the king about getting back her house and land.4 As she came in, the king was talking with Gehazi, the servant of the man of God. The king had just said, "Tell me some stories about the great things Elisha has done." 5 And Gehazi was telling the king about the time Elisha had brought a boy back to life. At that very moment, the mother of the boy walked in to make her appeal to the king about her house and land.

"Look, my lord the king!" Gehazi exclaimed. "Here is the woman now, and this is her son—the very one Elisha brought back to life!" 6 "Is this true?" the king asked her. And she told him the story. So he directed one of his officials to see that everything she had lost was restored to her, including the value of any crops that

had been harvested during her absence.

- *As we see in the story above, the preparation for restoration started whilst the woman was well and had not even lost anything . The first step was information.*

- *She was advised of what was to come:*

1. In this season, month and year, Lord, open my ears to crucial information that I need for the rest of the year.

2. You do not act without informing your precious ones, I receive updates that will prepare me to recover all that the enemy has stolen from me day by day through the rest of this season and year

- *There is the right timing to return*

3. Set an alarm in my spirit and cause me to stir when the set time for me to return to my possession is due.

- *This woman went to see the king the only authority who can give her what she has lost.*

4. Lord, give me an audience before they that can help me through this season month and year. My journeys do not have to be repeated many times to get result.

- *There are many people who are repeatedly being asked to come back   they keep asking you to come today, come tomorrow.*

5. This season month and year, every single journey will give me a hundred percent recovery in Jesus name.

6. Give me spokes-persons who will take on my issues as though they are their life's business raise for me tongues that will speak in my favour.

7. Prepare adverts for me speaking my good and preparing the grounds before I make demands off those who are holding the keys to my recovery.

8. Father, prior approval makes life easy, this season, month and year, direct my steps to every land and every platform where you have pre-approved me for ease.

- *The king asked the Shunamite woman - is this true?*

9. Lord, I receive the boldness to speak for my cause when faced with the opportunity to do so, to *be strong and take courage.* I receive the courage to explain my case before the appropriate through this season month and year.

- *The king assigned her to a general*

10. This season, month and year, I decree that I am assigned recovery specialists who will ease my way into a hundred percent recovery. Who is best to enforce a recovery than a man who has fought many wars? Lord, assign skilled personnel to my requests for recovery this month.

* The Shunamite woman had everything restored with interest added.

11. Lord, through this season, month and year, I recover all I've lost with interest added.

- *Whilst many were returning to start from the beginning, the Shunamite Woman was already operating from the position of advantage.*

12. Lord, in this season, month and year, ease of recovery will give me advantage where many are struggling to find their footing.

- *It was as though she never left.*

13. Lord, cause me to experience ease with recovery, that there will be no difference between my results and

those of they that never lost anything. I receive a commensurate catch-up.

- *Be careful to pray this if you are not ready for the result.*

14. It doesn't matter how long I have been cheated for, from this season, month and year, I declare restoration.

LUKE 15: 13-24

> *"Not long after that, the younger son got together all he had, set off for a distant country and there squandered his wealth in wild living.14 After he had spent everything, there was a severe famine in that whole country, and he began to be in need. 17 "When he came to his senses, he said, 'How many of my father's hired servants have food to spare, and here I am starving to death. 18 I will set out and go back to my father 19 I am no longer worthy to be called your son make me like one of your hired servants.' 20 So he got up and went to his father. "But while he was still a long way off, his father saw him and was filled with compassion for him he ran to his son, threw his arms around him and kissed him.22 "But the father said to his servants,*

'Quick! Bring the best robe and put it on him. Put a ring on his finger and sandals on his feet. 23 Bring the fattened calf and kill it. Let's have a feast and celebrate. 24 For this son of mine was dead and is alive again he was lost and is found.' So, they began to celebrate.

- *So, he got up and went to his father. "While he was still a long way off, his father saw him and was moved with compassion. His father ran to him, hugged him, and kissed him.*

15. Lord, today, I ask for mercy for wherever I have gone wrong and put myself in a position to be oppressed and plundered.

- *When God steps in, compassion makes those rightfully or legally holding unto our blessings to restore them to us.*

16. Lord, step into my case by yourself, showing me supernatural compassion that will lead to restoration.

17. Father, they that are due to restore my possessions, cause them to have compassion on me.

- *Ease gives access to what you should struggle and*

suffer to recover the prodigal son had lost his chance. Left to his brother, he was expected to sweat drops of blood before he would have access to anything great in life, but the God who ordained ease, got him restored before he even opened his mouth...

18. Beyond what the world thinks, I deserve and request to be restored to better than what I lost.

19. By human judgement, I deserve no good, but God, let your compassion open the doors of restoration to my household.

20. They that will restore, start to run to me with open arms this season, month and through the year in the name of Jesus.

21. Contrary to the difficulty that I have signed for, Lord, let your mercy bring me ease of restoration

22. Father, give them urgency to deal with my restoration.

- *Some women are not able to conceive because they walked out of God's mandate for holiness.*

23. Today, we obtain mercy and compassion on your account

- *Some families are in lack because the head of the home has gone against godly instructions. They have defiled the marital bed - for this reason, the enemy has taken prosperity away from their hands.*

24. Today, we ask for restoration according to god's mercy and compassion .

1 Samuel 30:1-2, 6-8, 16-19 AMP

> *Now it happened when David and his men came to Ziklag on the third day, [they found] that the Amalekites had made a raid on the Negev and on Ziklag, and had overthrown Ziklag and burned it with fire and they had taken captive the women [and all] who were there, both small and great. They killed no one but carried them off [to be used as slaves] and went on their way. Further, David was greatly distressed because the people spoke of stoning him, for all of them were embittered, each man for his sons and daughters. But David felt strengthened and encouraged in the Lord his God. David inquired of the Lord , saying, "Shall I pursue this band [of raiders]? Will I overtake them?" And He answered him, "Pursue, for you will certainly overtake them, and you will certainly rescue [the*

captives]. " *When he brought David down, the Amalekites had disbanded and spread over all the land, eating and drinking and dancing because of all the great spoil they had taken from the land of the Philistines and from the land of Judah. Then David [and his men] struck them down [in battle] from twilight until the evening of the next day and not a man of them escaped, except four hundred young men who rode camels and fled. So,David recovered all that the Amalekites had taken, and rescued his two wives. Nothing of theirs was missing whether small or great, sons or daughters, spoil or anything that had been taken David recovered it all.*

* *There are times when the thief steals just for the fun of it - the bible says they killed no one, just took them off as slaves. Why did they burn their dwelling? It was to prevent them from having anywhere to return to. There are afflictions that don't kill you but make you wish that you were dead that was what happened to David. It challenged his pride, dignity and glory as a man. What kind of a man had his whole family plundered under his nose*

1.   Father, I possess the gates of this season, month and

year and I disallow every oppression that will make my family wish they were dead.

26. That which makes me relevant, but has been taken away unlawfully, this season, month and year, I decree they shall be restored to me.

27. That which gave me joy, but was stolen from me in my moment of ignorance, I decree they be returned to me.

28. I bring to an abrupt end, everywhere, any celebration that originated from my captivity.

29. Every gathering that is scheduled to make mockery of me in this state of affliction, Lord, I bring judgement and condemnation upon them.

- *Recovery sometimes means that you must go to war.*

30. Lord strengthen my arms to confront those who have stolen from me. I receive boldness to challenge my oppressors this season, month and year, in the name of Jesus

- *Both David and the prodigal son got to a point where they were both distressed. David decided to get up in spite of the challenges   the prodigal son decided to get up despite his mistakes.*

- *The Shunamite woman decided to get up. No matter what was stolen from you, if you don't get up, and chase after the looters, it may be lost forever. This means that even though God has promised restoration, you still need to get up and take the steps towards re-possession.*

- *Do not be afraid of their faces through this season, this month and this year:*

30. I will set my face like a flint and walk back into territories which have been taken from me unlawfully and i shall recover all.

Congratulations on your prayers today I declare that all that you have struggled and laboured before you achieved in previous years, from this season month and year will now come to you on a platform of ease.

CHAPTER 4:
EASE OF INCREASE

Jacob had been serving for a while, but he needed to move to the next height unfortunately, he could not attain that next level without any substance. He had served, he had paid his dues, but they that were meant to pay him for services were now starting to play games. Jacob needed a formula that will work well while he was still righteous enough to stay in God's good books he needed something that will give him what he deserved, that which will get his due pay without committing a sin.

Genesis 30:25-43 (MSG)

After Rachel had Joseph, Jacob spoke to Laban, "Let me go back home. Give me my wives and children for whom I've served you. You know how hard I've worked for you." Laban said, "If you please, I have learned through divine inquiry that God has blessed me because of you." He went on, "So name your wages. I'll pay you." Jacob replied, "You know well what my work has meant to you and how your livestock has flourished under my care. The little you had when I arrived has increased greatly everything I did resulted in blessings for you. Isn't it about time that I do something for my own family?" "So, what should I pay you?"

Jacob said, "You don't have to pay me a thing. But how about this? I will go back to pasture and care for your flocks. Go through your entire flock today and take out every speckled or spotted sheep, every dark-coloured lamb, every spotted or speckled goat. They will be my wages. That way you can check on my honesty when you assess my wages. If you find any goat that's not speckled or spotted or a sheep that's not black, you will know that I stole it." "Fair enough," said Laban. "It's a deal." But that very day Laban removed all the mottled and spotted Billy goats and all the speckled and spotted nanny goats, every animal that had even a touch of white on it plus all the black sheep and placed them under the care of his sons. Then he put a three-day journey between himself and Jacob. Meanwhile Jacob went on tending what was left of Laban's flock. But Jacob got fresh branches from poplar, almond, and plane trees and peeled the bark, leaving white stripes on them. He stuck the peeled branches in front of the watering troughs where the flocks came to drink. When the flocks were in heat, they came to drink and mated in front of the streaked branches. Then they gave birth to young that were streaked or spotted or speckled. Jacob placed the ewes before the dark-coloured animals of

POSSESSING THE GATE

Laban. That way he got distinctive flocks for himself which he didn't mix with Laban's flocks. And when the sturdier animals were mating, Jacob placed branches at the troughs in view of the animals so that they mated in front of the branches. But he wouldn't set up the branches before the feebler animals. That way the feeble animals went to Laban and the sturdy ones to Jacob. The man got richer and richer, acquiring huge flocks, lots and lots of servants, not to mention camels and donkeys.

Genesis 30:27 (CEB)

Laban said to him, "Do me this favour. I've discovered by a divine sign that the LORD has blessed me because of you,

- *Not everyone will be an employer, some will be employee, but even as an employee, you can experience increase when employers suddenly realize that without you their business will fail.*

1. Lord, open the eyes of those I serve to see my relevance to their success.

2. The gift (endowment) of a man makes way for him.

Lord, let my uniqueness earn me ease of outstanding increase.

3. A man who is blind to his skills and uniqueness is a man who will remain a slave. Lord, through this season, month and year, open my eyes to see the keys to wealth and increase which have been handed to me.

4. I terminate every short term and long-standing appointment with all who have been benefiting from me without giving me due reward and honour.

5. I put an end to my contract with all they that wish to stylishly continue to harvest from my sweat, and usurp my destiny. They will suddenly do away with me....or I with them.

- *Some people were offered jobs several years ago, after the initial compliance they have now refused to make good their promise to give you your entitlement. Some retain your services or enter into business deals with you, but don't pay.*

6. Today, I take away the peace of every employer, business partner who has cheated me I decree that in this season, month and year, they will frantically seek

POSSESSING THE GATE 43

me and release my remuneration to me.

- *Laban said - Name your price as seen in:*

Genesis 30:27-28

27 *"Please listen to me," Laban replied. "I have become wealthy, for the LORD has blessed me because of you. 28 Tell me how much I owe you. Whatever it is, I'll pay it."*

- *Boldness to negotiate a favourable portion.*

7. Lord, from today, I receive insight to evaluate my worth properly, so I will not be cheated or short-changed.

8. Withdraw confidence and the tenacity to contend from my oppressors and usurpers so they have no confidence to argue with me.

- *Sometimes, businesses and organizations go the extra mile just to retain one person whilst no one is looking for other non-important people even though they are still as qualified.*

9. Whatever Jacob asked, he was too good to be turned down his impact was too much. This season, month and year, I receive wisdom to negotiate wealthy contracts

that will bring me increase

- *When a man's ways are pleasing to the lord, he makes even his enemies to be at peace with him.*

- *Laban had to agree*

10. Lord, they who will enrich me in this season, month and year, give them no alternatives to blessing me, they will have no choice but to bless me.

- *Laban changed figures, he removed the striped and spotted animals just because Jacob said that was what he wanted.*

11. Lord, it doesn't matter how hard they try to cheat me out of my entitlements, they will meet with failure

12. I Pray that this season, month and year, that a little will become a lot!!!

- *Whatever Jacob achieved under Laban remains in Laban's household until Jacob moved out. Freedom and room to increase if you increase and there is no room to break forth , it turns to hardship.*

13. Lord, I need room to increase I receive room to

expand on every side.

Proverbs 22:29

Seest thou a man diligent - Jacob was attentive enough to know that the sheep mated when they drank, some people will do their job so grudgingly that they wouldn't have noticed.

14. Help me lord to give attention to the tiny details that will enrich me in month.

- *He put the striped poles when the strong animals mated - wow! A workman is worthy of his wages Luke 10:7*

15. I receive peculiar instructions that will guide me to recover all losses from everywhere I have been cheated,

- *Jacob did not put the trees up when the weak ones mated, he planned his outcomes because of this, the man Jacob became very rich and strong....he did not have to suffer the suffering of Laban, we know that one sick animal can contaminate the rest.*

16. Lord, help me to choose only that which will make me

rich and add no sorrow in my selection process.

- *Jacob did not have to do more work, he kept doing what he was doing but then he got better reward.*

16. By virtue of supernatural insight, wealth will be allocated to me in this season, this month and year.

- *Increase brings enmity-* **Genesis 31:1**

17. Lord, expose them and warn me to steer clear of friends who will turn to enemies as you enlarge my coasts

Genesis 31:7

> *"if you have been cheated, and without sin, table your case before God   there is ease for increase in the house tonight"*

18. In this season, month and year, my resources will not enter the hands of the dwindler   Laban was a dwindler. He valued money more than his integrity. It's a heart full of sorrow to work with such people. *Genesis 31:14*

19. Lord, in this season, month and year, you will hinder me from joining business with the evil and crafty minded people.

Genesis 31:24,29

24   *Then God came to Laban the Aramean in a dream at night and said to him, "Be careful not to say anything to Jacob, either good or bad."*

* God warned and cautioned Laban

20.   Lord I give you permission to sound a harsh warning to they who have chosen to pursue me and cheat me to the point of distress.

21.   Getting an increase alone is not enough, there is a need to maintain the wealth. As the Lord increases me, the wealth he gives me will not take away the place of godly alignment in my life

Exodus 12:35-36 (CEV)

The Israelites had already done what Moses had told them to do. They had gone to their Egyptian neighbours and asked for gold and silver and for clothes. The lord had made the Egyptians friendly toward the people of Israel, and they gave them whatever they asked for. In this way they carried away the wealth of the Egyptians when they left Egypt.

- *God told you to go ask for something that he doesn't want you to return.*

Exodus 12:35-36(NIV)

> *The Israelites did as Moses instructed and asked the Egyptians for articles of silver and gold and for clothing. 36 The LORD had made the Egyptians favourably disposed toward the people, and they gave them what they asked for   so, they plundered the Egyptians.*

22. Lord, let me reason the way you reason and see the way you see   help me to follow your plans that will connect me to my much-needed increase

- *Isaac sowed in the land, but they started to attack his water wells, the source of nourishment for his flock. He then had to take his attention off increasing and began focusing on starting all over   this is wastage!*

25. Every little opening that the enemy has used to drain me, which has made it difficult for me to record increase today, I block them in Jesus name.

- *"You cannot increase if there is no rest. Suddenly, an established man started moving around every so often because his rest was threatened."*

26. Rest will not elude me this season, month, or year rest and increase go hand in hand. Through-out my life, I shall experience peace and rest, so that increase will come to me without stress.

- *"Isaac suffered in the hands of total strangers" "Jacob and his son suffered in the hands of close relatives."*

27. Father, in this season, month and years, whether relatives or strangers, none shall suffer me or deprive me my ease of increase.

Exodus 3:21-22

> *And I will give this people favour in the sight of the Egyptians: and it shall come to pass, that, when ye go, ye shall not go empty: 22. But every woman shall borrow of her neighbour, and of her that sojourneth in her house, jewels of silver, and jewels of gold, and raiment: and ye shall put them upon your sons, and upon your daughters and ye shall spoil the Egyptians.*

- *The favour of God makes people give us what they would*

not have given.

- *The Israelites were given gold etc.*

28. Lord, in this season month and year, because of your favour, I will not go empty.

29. Lord, I receive valuable gifting which will enrich me for generations to come.

I decree increase by heavenly according to the words of your prayer and in line with the word of God, that ease shall locate you wherever you are in the name of Jesus.

CHAPTER 5:
EASE OF APPOINTMENT

Many of us appear to have skills and are looking for how the skills will get us a financial reward   for some meanwhile, the remuneration is looking for them. Many employers go out of their way to seek these people because of the uniqueness of what they carry. This season, month and year, God says that before we labour, we will receive allocation to fat inheritance that will enrich us.

Daniel 1:3-7

One day the king ordered Ashpenaz, his highest palace official, to choose some young men from the royal family of Judah and from other leading Jewish families. 4 the king said, "they must be healthy, handsome, smart, wise, educated, and fit to serve in the royal palace. Teach them how to speak and write our language 5 and give them the same food and wine that I am served. Train them for three years, and then they can become court officials."6 four of the young Jews chosen were Daniel, Hananiah, Mishael, and Az-Ariah, all from the tribe of Judah. 7 but the king's chief official gave them Babylonian names: Daniel became Belteshazzar, Hananiah became Shadrach, Mishael became Meshach, and Azariah became Abednego.

- *These young men were removed forcefully from their own cities and from amongst their people they were taken away into slavery. The destination was to a foreign land and this must have been distressing for them. However, what they did not know was that this was a relocation for allocation it was designed to give them an access which they would not have had, if they had remained in their home country. If only we realize why God allows breaking-away and dislocation, we will embrace every painful change that God brings our way.*

1. Lord, forcefully disconnect me from long standing and chronic habitations which have subdued me and hindered me from performing at my best.

2. Some dislodging will be painful. Lord, please help me to see why you are moving me from my comfort zones to new and unfamiliar grounds of greater heights.

- *Captives are made to serve, they are slaves, but these four men and others taken with them, were singled out. This shows us that we don't have to suffer what others suffer even when we find ourselves in a predicament similar to theirs.*

3. Lord, despite the low tides of progress everywhere, you will single me out for recognition throughout this season, month and year.

- *God does not perform magic, He works miracles, that means instead of saying abracadabra, He will help you to equip yourself with what you need to stand out*

4. Father, help me sharpen my skills, so that I will have the access that I require for great places in life.

5. Help me to work towards the recognition that I desire. There are lessons I need to learn. Father, awaken my senses to meet the requirement needed for my next level.

- *There is a decorum and a composure that is befitting of a high achiever in life's circle.*

6. Father, put fire in my bones and cause me to push myself to be the best that I can be.

- *The king was looking for men who were the very best, he wanted men from the royal family who were outstanding in their performance. The boys were singled out and prepared for the life the king wanted them to live. Once they were fed by the king's menu, they were at his mercy. Their thinking faculty would be restricted, and their life choices cloned. "there is a meal that brings one to the same level as everyone else," It is called contamination. Righteousness exalts a nation.*

- *A few months ago, whilst hubby was ministering to a gentleman who had been looking for a job, he advised him that God will give him a job soon, but he needed to stay away from contamination. A few weeks down the line, he had a successful interview and his immediate senior was the first person to make a demand towards corruption. 'Give me some free diesel for my car', the manager said. The young man declined, not knowing that the overall manager was observing. That is the way to be promoted, righteousness exalts.*

6.   Father, sharpen my antenna to recognize compromise and contamination that will relegate me from supernatural to ordinary.

- *As seen in the book of Daniel.*

Daniel 1:15-16,19 (NCV)

After ten days, they looked healthier and better fed than

all the young men who ate the king's food. So the guard took away the king's special food and wine, feeding them vegetables instead. The king talked to them and found that none of the young men were as good as Daniel, Hananiah, Mishael, and Azariah. So those four young men became the king's servants.

- *"what will feed others may kill you, because what you carry is different from what they carry"*

8. Lord, I receive an appetite for excellence, which will nourish me for great insights.

Daniel 2:3, 5-6 (NCV)

Then the king said to them, "I had a dream that bothers me, and I want to know what it means." King Nebuchadnezzar said to them, "I meant what I said. You must tell me the dream and what it means. If you don't, I will have you torn apart, and I will turn your houses into piles of stones. But if you tell me my dream and its meaning, I will reward you with gifts and great honour. So, tell me the dream and what it means."

- *The king changed his plans to exclude other contenders! he wanted a meaning initially. A few moments later, he requested them to tell the dream and to also interpret it. He changed his requirements, even when there had been no change in the current situation!!!*

9. Lord, update the requirements of my benefactors to exclude my contenders, make room for my gifts.

Daniel 2:9 (NCV)

> *If you don't tell me my dream, you will be punished. You have all agreed to tell me lies and wicked things, hoping things will change. Now, tell me the dream so that I will know you can tell me what it really means!"*

- *These were the men whose opinions and interpretations had been respected in the land for many years before the arrival of these foreigners. Suddenly, they were receiving death threats.*

10. Cause my competitors to lose face and favour before my benefactors.

11. Father upgrade the terms and conditions by which success is accessed, to my favour.

Daniel 2:10-11 (NCV)

> *The wise men answered the king, saying, "no one on*

earth can do what the king asks! No great and powerful king has ever asked the fortune-tellers, magicians, or wise men to do this   the king is asking something that is too hard. Only the gods could tell the king, but the gods do not live among people."

12. Cause my benefactors to change their operational standards to align with my expertise, gifts and skills.

13. I activate all that you have equipped me with, that I need to live as gods amongst men.

- *The men in the city said, "only the gods can do this!"*

14. Lord, from now on, confirm my supernatural skills before men.

- *Daniel called for prayer back up.*

15. Lord, I receive the wisdom needed to take every step I need to take that will propel me into supernatural limelight.

Daniel 2:22 (NCV)

He makes known secrets that are deep and hidden he knows what is hidden in darkness, and light is all around him.

16. Lord, I receive keys to deep and hidden secrets, that will give me solutions that will shock the world around me

Daniel 2:46 (NCV)

> *Then king Nebuchadnezzar fell face down on the ground in front of Daniel. The king honoured him and commanded that an offering and incense be presented to him.*

13. In this season, month and year, kings will fall at my feet in honour of the gift of God upon my life.

Daniel 2:48

> *Then the king gave Daniel many gifts plus an important position in his kingdom. Nebuchadnezzar made him ruler over the whole area of Babylon and put him in charge of all the wise men of Babylon.*

- *The gift of a man makes way for him - Proverbs 18:16*

18. Lord, I receive that gift that will open the gates to many more gifts.

19. Lord, give me a position that will make they that disregard me have no choice but to acknowledge your

special gift in my life.

Daniel 2:48-49 (MSG)

- *Then the king promoted Daniel to a high position in the kingdom, lavished him with gifts, and made him the governor over the entire province of Babylon and the chief in charge of all the Babylonian wise men. At Daniel's request the king appointed Shadrach, Meshach, and Abednego to administrative posts throughout Babylon, while Daniel governed from the royal headquarters.*

- *Who wouldn't appoint Daniel, a man to whom God reveals secrets?*

20. Lord, give me what the world needs that will put me on the world map for recognition in my chosen career.

- *Daniel did not ask for his own appointment, the king thought it wise to appoint him.*

21. Father, I receive supernatural adverts that will make men appoint me to great places without applying or soliciting.

- *The three Hebrew men met with Daniel who requested*

their appointment even though they didn't lobby. The destinies of many are attached to mine and mine to some others.

22. Lord, set me up with contacts/associates who will enforce my promotion and make it their duty to ensure I get my allocation in high places.

Daniel 3:24, 26 - 26, 29 (MSG)

Suddenly, king Nebuchadnezzar jumped up in alarm and said, "didn't we throw three men, bound hand and foot, into the fire?" "that's right, o king," They said. Nebuchadnezzar went to the door of the roaring furnace and called in, ", servants of the high god, come out here!" Shadrach, Meshach, and Abednego walked out of the fire. "therefore, I issue this decree: Anyone anywhere, of any race, colour, or creed, who says anything against the god of Shadrach, Meshach, and Abednego will be ripped to pieces, limb from limb, and their houses torn down. There has never been a god who can pull off a rescue like this."

- *To be appointed is not just enough, even the appointment has to be secure.*

- *With success, appointments and promotions come enmity the same soothsayers who could not interpret dreams were now the ones making suggestions to the king. They planned to discredit Daniel and the three Hebrew young men.*

23. Lord, secure me all round, as I enjoy divine attention in my appointment.

- *The wise men tried to implicate the four Hebrew men, unfortunately, the Hebrew men increased in number instead of burning up in the fiery furnace.*

24. Lord, you will persistently back me up in the new appointment and deliver me from the schemes of men.

25. Lord, in this season, month and year, my contenders will have no choice but to ask me in awe how I have managed to stay on top and my answer will be, if it had not been for the lord on my side, where will we be?

26. Lord, in this season, month and year, what generations before me were unable to achieve due to limitations, you will allocate to me on a platform of ease.

I decree increase by heavenly mandate according to the words of your prayer and in line with the word of God, that ease shall locate you wherever you are in the name of Jesus.

CHAPTER 6:
EASE OF SUPERNATURAL REMEMBRANCE

Many times, we don't get what we deserve in life, because people forget. Other times, we don't get what we desire, because we just need a supernatural wave to blow in our direction to hasten things up a bit.

God's word for everyone joining in this prayer is that we will be remembered, and this will trigger a cascade which has been abandoned for years.

- *Remember yourself*

- *Some people don't need to be remembered they only need to remember themselves. If life seems to have shifted you from hopeful to hopeless all you need is just to remember who you are.*

- *Everything God has deposited in you was meant to make life easy, but the enemy has stolen from you or taken away your confidence in your endowment.*

- *If you had a car at home, but forget the keys at home and set out on a journey, you will struggle like one who doesn't own a car. The prodigal son came to his senses when he remembered who he was.*

1. Father, you created me with ease in mind, I ask that

you awaken my memory to whom you created me to be, that every malfunctioning will cease in this season, month and year in Jesus name

2. Every greatness that you designed in my being which I have abandoned and forgotten due to lack of use or stimulation, Father, through this season, month and year, remind me and re-instate me.

3. Lord, in this season, month and year, I come back to my senses and reclaim all that I am which the enemy had taken the details away due to moments of hardship.

4. Lord, please restore me to and help me, not only to chase after, but to recover myself so that my ease will be obvious.

- *Remembered by others*

  Biblical example of people who were remembered in the bible

- *Mordecai the lord took away the sleep of the king*

- *The good works you did years ago that did not yield any reward will suddenly be brought into the limelight .*

- *Mordecai just didn't get remembered, someone stood at the gates to make a declaration. Today, we will stand in the gap for ourselves and our households.*

5. Father, every workman and work-woman is worthy of their wages. Every labour which I and my spouse have put in which has gone without recognition for years no matter how far back it goes, I call them to the memory of those who have benefited from us and I command that in this season, month and year, a cascade of compensation that will usher me into ease will start straight away.

6. Every good I have done, which has gone unnoticed and unrewarded before now, I assign angels of the lord, to start juggling the memory of those I have helped, to remember my actions and speedily reward me with everything that I need for my ease.

7. There are people who need to feel uncomfortable, before they can think properly, every mind, whose peaceful state has made my past toils and effort to go

unnoticed, today, I withhold your peace and decree that God will start to bring situations your way that will highlight my past services and roles. You will feel discomfort until you reach the point of action to usher me into ease.

8. Father let my oppressors make mistakes that will expose their wickedness and put an end to my hardship, unease and disease.

   Even when men remember, they need to act. They need to take active steps based on their quickened memory.

Esther 2:1

   After these things, when the wrath of king Ahasuerus was appeased, he remembered Vashti, and what she had done, and what was decreed against her. 2. Then said the king's servants that ministered unto him, let there be fair young virgins sought for the king.

9. Everyone meant to do me good, and bring me ease, as you remember me, you will act. I cancel every counsel that will make you disregard the prompting of the lord.

10. I silence every adviser who will wrongfully allocate my reward of the present, past and the future labour to

another, thereby prolonging my difficulty

11. All those whom I have served will find it impossible to forget my labour and will move with speed to give me my entitlement that will usher me into ease.

Job 14: 7-9

> *"for there is hope for a tree—if it's cut down, it sprouts again and grows tender, new branches. 8-9 though its roots have grown old in the earth, and its stump decays, it may sprout and bud again at the touch of water, like a new seedling.*

- *God says there is hope if God allowed that to be written in the bible, it's for a reason. A workman is worthy of his wages.*

12. Father, everywhere that I have left dried up traces and drops of my sweat where I have been disgraced and dismissed without due recognition, right now, I decree that the dew of heaven will start to activate my sweat and cause budding that will produce big rewards for me to enjoy

13. Even the ones that have experienced decay, Lord, the dry bones rose and the flesh that has long decayed

received life at your word, so tonight, that same power that quickened the dead tissues in *Ezekiel 37*, I command you to go into my path in life and resurrect all my labour and cause them to demand a due reward that will usher me into ease.

14. The same thing that applies to labour applies to body part for my ease to be complete, I decree every body part that has been reported to have stopped functioning and now left for the dead, at the touch of the dew of heaven upon me through this season, month and year, you will receive life and be restored to newness. The seeds which seem to have died will resurrect, ovaries declared menopausal will revive.

15. Ease is when you don't have to repeat the work before you get the due enjoyment. When the flesh and bones came to life, they did not need to be taught, they knew where to go, without me making any extra effort in this season, month and year, my efforts which have laid dormant for years will start to yield increase on their own accord.

- *God remembered Noah -*

Genesis 8:1 (CJB)

> *God remembered Noah*, every living thing and all the livestock with him in the ark   so God caused a wind to pass over the earth, and the water began to go down.*

- *The land that was water-logged dried up gradually, the question is this: Why was the earth waterlogged?It was not Noah's fault   But Noah was the one held in a container going nowhere.*

- *Flooding brings disease, Noah's children malfunctioned, I bet the developed post-traumatic stress disorder   another question is this - Why would anyone choose to rape their father?*

16. Lord, when I look around me, all that I see is a mess that is not my fault   remember me today and kick start my journey towards recovery of all that I have lost.

17. What I have lost was worth years of sweats and labour, Father, remember me and settle me on a new ground to recover without chaos, bringing me ease.

18. When God remembered Noah, he sent a wind   wind alone does dry up, but science says wind needs heat to

work quicker. Lord send heated wind to begin to shift things into position in my life in through this season, month and year.

19. The wind parted the red sea, Lord, as you remember me in this season, month and year, every journey which I was meant to make but has been hindered, as you remember me, the wind of your breath will part ways for me in a way that none has ever experienced before.

- *God remembered Rachel*

Genesis 30:22

- *Then God remembered Rachel's plight and answered her prayers by enabling her to have children.*

  When the oppressors are having a field day, then God remembered Rachel and let her conceive. The Message version says God remembered her , God listened to her and opened her womb, if He did it then, He can do it again.

18. For the women and men trusting God for children, Lord, in this season, month and year, you God will

remember them, you will listen to them and open their womb.

- *God remembered Abraham and extended an arm of protection to they who matter to him, Lot.*

Genesis 19:29 (CEB)

> *When God destroyed the cities in the valley, God remembered Abraham and sent Lot away from the disaster that overtook the cities in which Lot had lived. 30 Since Lot had become fearful of living in Zoar, he and his two daughters headed up from Zoar and settled in the mountains where he and his two daughters lived in a cave. 31 The older daughter said to the younger, "Our father is old, and there are no men in the land to sleep with us as is the custom everywhere.*

- *When God destroyed the cities in the valley, god remembered Abraham and sent lot away from the disaster that overtook the cities in which lot had lived.*

19. Lord, in this season, month and year, because you will remember me, it doesn't matter who is dying or being destroyed, you will preserve all them that matter to me.

- *God remembered Hannah*

- *The Message Bible puts it well:*

1 Samuel 1:19-20 (MSG)

> *Up before dawn, they worshipped god and returned home to Ramah. Elkanah slept with Hannah his wife, and god began making the necessary arrangements in response to what she had asked. Before the year was out, Hannah had conceived and given birth to a son. She named him Samuel, explaining, "I asked God for him."*

20. God, please begin to make the necessary arrangements for all I have been asking.

- *Mephibosheth was remembered.*

2 Samuel 8:1-7

> *One day David asked, "is there anyone left of Saul's family? If so, I'd like to show him some kindness in honour of Jonathan." The king asked, "is there anyone left from the family of Saul to whom I can show some godly kindness?" Ziba told the king, "yes, there is Jonathan's son, lame in both feet." King David didn't*

lose a minute. He sent and got him from the home of makir son of Ammiel in lo debar. "don't be frightened," Said David. "I'd like to do something special for you in memory of your father Jonathan. To begin with, I'm returning to you all the properties of your grandfather Saul. Furthermore, from now on you'll take all your meals at my table."

- *What was the life of Mephibosheth? Crippled....not his fault, Deprived of the throne - not his fault, Out of place - not his fault.*

- *There are things that can be changed that will bring ease.*

2 Samuel 9:1,3-3,5,7 (MSG)

21. Father give people verbal diarrhoea and cause them to remember me and mention my name before they that will bring me the ease that I desire.

22. Lord, they that are carrying that which will bring me ease in this season, month and year will see a need for haste in settling my matter.

23. I call forth every good, every favour , every positive inheritance that has been owed to my generations

before me, to come to the memory of the custodians of my ease.

- *Joseph got remembered by the chief butler*

- *Joseph's journey through life entered a dark patch, not because he did anything wrong, but because someone hated him.*

Genesis 40:12

> *Joseph said, within three days, Pharaoh will get you out of here and put you back to your old work—you'll be giving Pharaoh his cup just as you used to do when you were his cup bearer only remember me when things are going well with you again—tell Pharaoh about me and get me out of this place. I was kidnapped from the land of the Hebrews. And since I've been here, I've done nothing to deserve being put in this hole." But the head cup bearer never gave Joseph another thought he forgot all about him.*

Genesis 40:12-15,23 (MSG)

24. In my journey through life, I have signed contracts which have been forgotten, or even contracts of ease signed by my parents, and ancestors, today, I awaken

such contracts and I decree that every custodian of such contract will wake up from slumber.

25. Father, introduce situations and circumstances into the lives of they who are scheduled to announce me, that they may remember me and fulfil their ordained destinies towards me

Genesis 41:9, 12-15,33,43-43,45 (CEB)

Then the chief wine steward spoke to Pharaoh: "Today I've just remembered my mistake. A young Hebrew man, a servant of the commander of the royal guard, was with us. We described our dreams to him, and he interpreted our dreams for us, giving us an interpretation for each dream. His interpretations came true exactly: So, Pharaoh summoned Joseph, and they quickly brought him from the dungeon. He shaved, changed clothes, and appeared before Pharaoh. Pharaoh said to Joseph, "now Pharaoh should find an intelligent, wise man and give him authority over the land of Egypt. He put Joseph on the chariot of his second-in-command, and everyone in front of him cried out, "Attention!" So, Pharaoh installed him over the entire land of Egypt. Pharaoh renamed Joseph, Zaphenath-paneah, and married him to Asnath, the daughter of Potiphera the priest of Heliopolis. Then Joseph assumed control of the land of Egypt.

26. In this season, month and year, following my announcement in places of importance, I shall be called upon to demonstrate my uniqueness which will usher me into ease.

- *Joseph was invited without asking into the presence of the same king that many would seek audience for.*

27. I open the doors to platforms that are unreachable to many to bring me ease without struggle and transform my destiny.

28. Lord, there are great vacancies awaiting my occupation, in this season, month and year, you will put me in the mind of they who will give a word that will ease my way into greatness, and this without dropping a sweat.

I decree increase by heavenly mandate according to the words of your prayer and in line with the word of God, that ease shall locate you wherever you are in the name of Jesus.

CHAPTER 7:
EASE OF MARITAL REWARD

1. Lord, every word, every comment, every submission I made in the past, which has ushered me into difficulty in my home, I repent today, and ask for your mercy to cover me.

Psalms 16:5-6 (CEB)

You, lord , are my portion, my cup   you control my destiny. The property lines have fallen beautifully for me   yes, I have a lovely home.

- *Yes, the lines are falling unto me in pleasant place.*

2. Lord, I am aware that the land which you allocated to me is a pleasant place, this season, month and year, I decree that everything that has made my land dry, cracked and bitter, I give you permission to remove and heal my land.

3. Every land that is meant to bring me nourishment but has brought me hard work and sorrow, Father, send the dew of heaven to soften and give me ease of productivity.

4. When the rain soaks the earth, tender roots grown into trees start to bud, Lord, send the rains of your mercy upon my inhabited land, that I may reap with

ease.

5. I declare that I have a place of solace in the home where you placed me lord.

6. I decree that my marred relationship will be joyous and fruitful.

7. I decree that this peace will also reign in their marriage, I shut the door to repetitive argument and selfish preoccupations

8. I decree that in this marriage, I will not be a victim of the tongues of men. My husband or wife, you shall not open me up to be oppressed by the tongues of men.

9. Every contact and friends or acquaintances currently keep, who may influence my husband, wife wrongly, stand as a distraction or deterrent from enjoying my marital destiny, Lord, I give you permission to put a separation between us.

- *To enjoy peace in marriage, you need to have sound judgement and godly assessment of situations.*

10. Lord, I shall see my husband or wife only through your eyes   so that my assessment of him or her shall

continually be right.

- *Some will labour with a spouse for 30 years, only to have peace after their death   they suddenly become nice when they have a few days to live as a result of a terminal condition   after suffering their spouse for many years, they are still nursed on their death bed by the same spouse.*

11. I am righteous and I bring forth my fruit in due season, Lord, all that is due me in marriage will come promptly. I shall not experience delay in getting my marital rewards.

- *If you become unwell, or husband becomes unwell, sexual intimacy becomes a secondary subject.*

12. In good and perfect health will I enjoy marital destiny   my body will not frustrate my marital fulfilment. My husband's or my wife's body will not frustrate my marital fulfilment.

13. Any exposures, interventions that may hinder me from being martially fruitful, today, I begin to order them out of your way in Jesus name.

14. I guard my home by God's love I guard me from invasion by the hand of the wicked. I secure my marital destiny away from manipulation.

15. I shall not be oppressed by strange men or women in my marital home anyone who is not fulfilling the purpose of God is strange, I keep them out of my home.

Song of songs 4:9-13,15 (NCV)

My sister, my bride, you have thrilled my heart you have thrilled my heart with a glance of your eyes, with one sparkle from your necklace. Your love is so sweet, my sister, my bride. Your love is better than wine, and your perfume smells better than any spice. My bride, your lips drip honey honey and milk are under your tongue. Your clothes smell like the cedars of Lebanon. My sister, my bride, you are like a garden locked up, like a walled-in spring, a closed-up fountain. Your limbs are like an orchard of pomegranates with all the best fruit, filled with flowers and, you are like a garden fountain— a well of fresh water flowing down from the mountains of Lebanon.

16. God's intention is for my husband or wife to be faithful to you. It is wickedness to take your body which the

lord says belongs to me and give to another husband or wife, you will find it impossible to be unfaithful to me.

17. My husband, your bodily members belong to me and I decree that they will not serve you in adultery.

18. My husband or wife, with the glance of my eyes, you shall be fulfilled.

19. You will find no delight in any other man or woman outside me.

20. Every contract you have signed, every agreement you entered into to nourish another and give them priority over me, today, because by marital covenant, you belong to me, I cancel such ungodly arrangement and covenant.

21. Every hidden or obvious commitment that you have entertained or intend to entertain or signed to prefer another above me or alongside me, I cancel right now in Jesus name.

22. Today, I renew the foundation of peace for this marriage, as we journey together, we will make choices and decisions that will help us to build on

peace. Great shall be your marital reward in Jesus name.

- *God is big on reward   Jesus sent the disciples out in twos.*

Ecclesiastes 4:9-12 (CEB)

> *Two are better than one because they have a good return for their hard work. If either should fall, one can pick up the other. But how miserable are those who fall and don't have a companion to help them up! Also, if two lie down together, they can stay warm. But how can anyone stay warm alone? Also, one can be overpowered, but two together can put up resistance. A three-ply cord doesn't easily snap.*

- *One of the purposes of marital partnership is that help is easily available   woe unto he who is alone when he falls, I am meant to have help in marriage....the help is supposed to support me when I am weak*

23. Lord I lay demand on the provision of help made for me through my husband or wife in this marriage.

24. You my husband or wife, will labour and do that is in your ability to help me.

25. You my husband or wife, when you identity my weakness and step in to rescue.

26. I am ordained to have support that will respond when I am in need, my husband or wife, you will not disregard or ignore me in my moment of need.

27. Your reward for your labour is also tied to my help, my husband or wife, you will joyfully step in and occupy your position in our relationship under God.

- *When you are alone, you can be easily overpowered.*

28. The plan of God is that because of marriage, my victories should be easier in the battles of life, my husband or wife, you will not expose me to defeat

I decree increase by heavenly mandate according to the words of your prayer and in line with the word of God, that ease shall locate you wherever you are in the name of Jesus.

CHAPTER 8:
EASE OF POSSESSION

To possess is to take ownership of something. To acquire a thing. Many times, in the bible, we see how God enabled his faithful to take ownership of things that he wanted them to have. God has proclaimed that in this season he will make ownership easy for his chosen people worldwide.

2 kings 7:5-9 (NLT)

So, at twilight they set out for the camp of the Arameans. But when they came to the edge of the camp, no one was there! For the lord had caused the Aramean army to hear the clatter of speeding chariots and the galloping of horses and the sounds of a great army approaching. "the king of Israel has hired the Hittites and Egyptians to attack us!" They cried to one another. So, they panicked and ran into the night, abandoning their tents, horses, donkeys, and everything else, as they fled for their lives. When the lepers arrived at the edge of the camp, they went into one tent after another, eating and drinking wine and they carried off silver and gold and clothing and hid it. Finally, they said to each other, "this is not right. This is a day of good news, and we aren't sharing it with anyone! If we wait until morning, some calamity will certainly fall upon us.

Come on, let's go back and tell the people at the palace."

- *Ease of possession can happen without the attendant struggle when the word of God has gone ahead of you. God made the enemies to develop auditory hallucinations, just so the chosen of the lord could possess the content of the land with ease.*

1. Lord, you have released a word to us for this season, month and year, so,I stand upon this word and I authorize you to cause a noise in the camp of the custodians of my possessions and cause them to panic in confusion and abandon every one of my possession within their hold in the name of Jesus.

2. Lord, there are results that are beyond my physical capabilities for now, but with your enablement, it's nothing but a walkover, Lord, I ask for you to supernaturally enable me beyond what my physical abilities can carry.

3. Lord, I receive and possess territories beyond my human sense in Jesus name.

4. Your word went ahead of the lepers, Lord, same scenario, same result. Your word has gone ahead of us,

so that in this season, month and year, we will have ease of possession.

It was the word you gave that started off a cascade of supernatural events. From the start of this season, month and year, Lord, by your word, start out a cascade of supernatural events that will get me uncommon access to territories.

5. In Medicine, what happened there is referred to as an "auditory hallucination" it causes a delusion, a strong unshakable idea. People start running when no one is chasing them.

6. Lord, for everyone who has resisted me with force, on my journey to your allocation, give them strong unshakable ideas that will in turn enrich me.

Number 13:27

> *This was their report to Moses: "we entered the land you sent us to explore, and it is indeed a bountiful country—a land flowing with milk and honey. Here is the kind of fruit it produces.*

•   *There are people whom when you spend 5 minutes with them, your dreams and aspirations are doomed immediately.*

7. Lord, send me a voice of encouragement that will see in me what I have not seen in myself and propel me towards my bountiful Countries.

8. Lord, send me enablers in this season, month and year, who will stand behind me to push me towards my allocated doors of possession.

- *No matter what anyone is seeing, if you don't see it, it's a waste of time.*

9. Lord, open my eyes to see the real value of that which you have allocated to me.

Numbers 27:2, 4-7 (NLT)

> *These women stood before Moses, Eleazar the priest, the tribal leaders, and the entire community at the entrance of the tabernacle. Why should the name of our father disappear from his clan just because he had no sons? Give us property along with the rest of our relatives." So, Moses brought their case before the lord. And the lord replied to Moses, "the claim of the daughters of Zelophehad is legitimate. You must give them a grant of land along with their father's relatives.*

Assign them the property that would have been given to their father.

10. Lord, I receive boldness to confront, question and demand my possessions from the hands of every usurper

- *Speaking right may make the difference between possession and denial.*

11. Lord, in the season, month and year, I shall speak right before the people who matter regarding my allocated destinies and territories.

12. Lord, in this season, month and year, I will not waste my efforts on lands that are not allocated to me.

Psalm 105:43-45 (MSG)

Remember this! He led his people out singing for joy his chosen people marched, singing their hearts out! He made them a gift of the country they entered, helped them seize the wealth of the nations so they could do everything he told them— could follow his instructions to the letter. Hallelujah!

13. Lord, turn every country I tread upon to a gift in my

possession.

14. Lord, in this season, month and year, please help me seize the wealth of the nations allocated to me.

15. The essence of the ease of possession is to make it easy to do what God has commanded, Lord, help me make obedience to you my priority, as you bless me.

Deuteronomy 11:22-25 (MSG)

> *That's right. If you diligently keep all this commandment that I command you to obey—love God, your God, do what he tells you, stick close to him— God on his part will drive out all these nations that stand in your way. Yes, he'll drive out nations much bigger and stronger than you. Every square inch on which you place your foot will be yours. Your borders will stretch from the wilderness to the mountains of Lebanon, from the Euphrates river to the Mediterranean Sea. No one will be able to stand in your way. Everywhere you go, god -sent fear and trembling will precede you, just as he promised.*

16. Borders will stretch, people will look and say "oh, we thought the cut-off point had already been specified

the last time we checked." Father, stretch boundaries, modify criteria, extend cut off points, make organizations bend all the way backwards and forward to accommodate me, and make them open doors of easy access to possession to me .

17. Every inch I walk, as long as I can walk, I can possess   Lord, give me the resilience that I need to keep walking.

18. Lord, give strength to my legs , so I may travel far claiming territories.

19. Lord, in this season, month and year, no one will be able to stand in my way, no man, woman, no authority, no government, no organization, no legal body, no individual, no corporate facility, no one will be able to stand in my way.

Nehemiah 9:25 (NLT)

> *They took over houses full of good things, with cisterns already dug and vineyards and olive groves and fruit trees in abundance. So, they ate until they were full and grew fat and enjoyed themselves in all your blessings.*

- *To take over, means that it was in the possession of*

someone else, .that means someone else has done the demanding, searching   you just walk in, they will say, it was just the person before you who put this in place.

20. Lord, this is my season to start to enjoy territories that have been pre-filled with good things.

21. Lord, in this season, month and year, I enjoy pre-approved access to great riches.

22. As I possess great riches and wealth in this season, month and year, I receive the wisdom and ability to enjoy the blessings.

Nehemiah 9:23,24

"then you helped our ancestors conquer kingdoms and nations, and you placed your people in every corner of the land. You made their descendants as numerous as the stars in the sky and brought them into the land you had promised to their ancestors. "they went in and took possession of the land. You subdued whole nations before them. Even the Canaanites who inhabited the land, were powerless! Your people could deal with these nations and their kings as they pleased. Our ancestors

captured fortified cities and fertile land.

23. Establish me by placing my people in decision making positions in every land.

- *We know that numbers can influence the psyche, even for the strong.*

24. Lord , give strength to my impact by making my reach wider.

Psalm 2:7-9 (CEB)

> *I will announce the lord 's decision: He said to me, "You are my son, today I have become your father. Just ask me, and I will make the nations your possession the far corners of the earth will be your property. You will smash them with an iron rod you will shatter them like a pottery jar."*

25. Lord, in this season, month and year, I have nations for my possession.

26. No man receives anything except they be given from above. Lord, you will dissuade every contender for my possession through this season, month and year, they will suddenly lose interest and back off.

27. Jacob kept digging wells, they belonged to him by right, but he couldn't flourish in spite of them. In this season, month and year, the God of heaven will frustrate every effort to deprive me of the joy I am entitled to from my possession.

28. Lord, I dispossess the inhabitants of every land that you have given me.

- *He left there and dug another well, but they didn't argue about it, so he named it Rehoboth and said, "Now the lord has made an open space for us and has made us fertile in the land." They said, "We now see that the lord was with you.*

29. They stopped arguing. In this season, month and year, those who argued with me and deprived me of my possessions will suddenly retreat permanently

I decree increase by heavenly mandate according to the words of your prayer and in line with the word of God, that ease shall locate you wherever you are in the name of Jesus.

102   POSSESSING THE GATE

CHAPTER 9:
EASE OF ACCESS

What you have access to decides where you go and what you will get. Many of us have been delayed because our access routes are blocked, and we have had to travel farther, looking for alternatives. Some are not delayed, they are totally denied, because there are no alternative routes to where they are trying to access.

For some other people, they have difficult access. What others get with ease, they will still get, but not all the entitlements. When they get there, they will have to labour harder before they can get the same result as others.

Many others can have some, but they cannot go all the way they can marry, but have no children.

For others, denial of access means that everything else is impossible. If you don't pass the driving test, you can't apply for the job. If you don't have the certification, you cannot be recommended for the next step. If you don't relocate to join your spouse, you can't start your family   denial of access in one aspect, puts life on hold in other aspects, access is restricted

For as many as will believe, from this season, month and year onwards, the doors of access which have shut in your face will start to open as you place a demand on them to do so, regardless of if they have been delayed, denied, difficult or restricted.

- Before we start, God says to warn you   His son had to be born in a manger, that's the prophecy. God had to protect His son, hide him from a public accredited place. Some access will be denied because God must protect you, and the fact that there was no space at the inn did not mean that God was not in the matter. Having noted this, we can now decree ease of access for the gates that God has freely given to us.

- Access to dominate

Isaiah 45: 1-3

Thus saith Jehovah to his anointed, to Cyrus, whose right hand I have holden, to subdue nations before him, and I will lose the loins of kings   to open the doors before him, and the gates shall not be shut: 2 I will go before thee, and make the rough places smooth ii will break in pieces the doors of brass, and cut in sunder the bars of iron 3 And I will give thee the treasures of darkness, and hidden riches of secret places, that thou mayest know that it is , Jehovah.

- *The bible says - be fruitful multiply, replenish the earth, .dominate and subdue it   how can you dominate what you don't have access to.*

    What I love about this scripture is that the only criteria for enjoying this ease of access is for you to have a personal relationship with God, so, if you don't know God through Jesus, and He doesn't know you, you may want to ask him into your life before we get too far into this .

Isaiah 45:1 - 2 (CEV)

    The Lord said to Cyrus, his chosen one   I have taken hold of your right hand to help you capture nations and remove kings from power. City gates will open for you not one will stay closed. As i lead you, i will level mountains and break the iron bars on bronze gates of cities.

1. Lord, I am your anointed, take hold of my right hand today so I may capture the nations that have escaped my reach before now, mention the nations that have escaped your reach before now.

2. Because the lord is holding my hands, every king,

whose decrees have made it impossible for me to access my cities of possession, today I unseat you from power.

- *If you are being chased and you have to arrive home late at night, you will appreciate the benefit of an electric gate that you can open and shut by pressing a button inside your car, It gives you added security and makes your arrival effortless.*

3. Lord, for ease of access to my promised land, I receive your supernatural help to smoothen rough places prior to my arrival. I don't just want access, I want a smooth one.

- *When the rain has fallen, even weak roots find it easy to draw life from the grounds.*

4. I receive watered grounds that will precede my arrival and give me ease of access to what will nourish me and bring me growth.

- *Mountains are very high, when you have been travelling for long, and you are tired, climbing them is a chore.*

5. Lord, no matter how close to the breakthrough, when

one cannot see it, it is discouraging, send help for me that will assist me and cheer me up on my journey towards my access.

6. As I unseat kings who have made unfavourable decrees towards my access, I decree that the city gates start to fling open to receive me and reward me.

- *Many people travel abroad and for years, they struggle. Then others arrive later and overtake them that means early arrival does not always give advantage. What they have access to is what makes the difference.*

7. As the city gates give me access, I receive speed to catch up and recover all that I have lost as a result of delay.

- *As I lead you, I will break the iron bars on bronze gates of cities, these gates are there to stop progress. When you meet bronze gates(bronze is harder than pure iron and far more resistant to corrosion) that means it can be there for several generations and not be exposed to weathering. It can last indefinitely, they are heavy, but when the bronze gates are fortified with iron bars, your case is hopeless, because the likelihood of you having access is almost non-existent.*

8.   Lord, as you lead me in this season, month and year, every fortified strong gate which has denied me access to my cities, I ask that you begin to break them asunder for me.

- *At times, people require something of you in exchange for access. Then when you give up what was requested, they require more and more things from you each time you fulfil the last demand.*

9.   Every multi-level hindrance that unfolds as I journey towards greatness, today, and for the rest of the year, I bring you to an end and decree my permanent access to ease.

Access to deliverance

- *Even if you can swim, there are waters that you know were not designed for you to swim through, they are too wide and too deep, simply because, the further you go, the more likely you are to run out of steam, hope deferred makes the heart weary.*

- *Waters that are deep and boisterous, waters that historically wasted many mean-while, they need to cross the waters to get to the other side.*

Exodus 14:10 , 13 - 16 , 21 - 22 , 24 - 25 , 29 (CEB)

As Pharaoh drew closer, the Israelites looked back and saw the Egyptians marching toward them. The Israelites were terrified and cried out to the lord . But Moses said to the people, "Don't be afraid. Stand

Stand your ground and watch the lord rescue you today. The Egyptians you see today you will never ever see again. The lord will fight for you. You just keep still." Then the lord said to Moses, "Why do you cry out to me? Tell the Israelites to get moving. As for you, lift your shepherd's rod, stretch out your hand over the sea, and split it in two so that the Israelites can go into the sea on dry ground. Then Moses stretched out his hand over the sea. The lord pushed the sea back by a strong east wind all night, turning the sea into dry land. The waters were split into two. The Israelites walked into the sea on dry ground. The waters formed a wall for them on their right hand and on their left.

Lord, whatever has terrified me before today, I stand my ground and prepare for a confrontation that will lead to permanent deliverance in and through this season, month and year. You know what has kept you in bondage to fear, mention it now, and deal with it.

10. The bible says the Egyptians you see today, you shall see no more, I decree thus, that every force of oppression that has limited me from having access to freedom, from today, I shall see you no more.

11. The lord says tell them to start moving father, I receive the instruction for the next step that will enforce my access.

12. As Moses obeyed, the Lord himself pushed the sea back by a strong east wind. Lord, as I obey you in and through this season month and year, you will send your strong wind to dry up every river that has hindered me.

13. Lord, from this season, month and year onwards, I walk into the level of ease of access that has never accessed by anyone before, in the history of my career.

14. Lord, from this season, month and year onwards, I decree the failure of every brass gates that have defied corrosion and maintained its integrity in my family line for generations.

15. From this season, month and year onwards, everything created by God, every natural element will work together with me to give me ease of access and give me an advantage over my detractors.

I Decree that:

- *The rain will soften my hard, dry land.*

- *The wind will sweep away years of dust that has covered doors leading to my treasured.*

- *The sun will dry up waterlogged lands that have made my feet heavy and slowed down my pace.*

- *The waters will come in the way and restrict my oppressors and contenders.*

- *Access to Territories*

Joshua 6:1 - 4, 16, 20 (GNT)

The gates of Jericho were kept shut and guarded to keep the Israelites out. No one could enter or leave the city. The lord said to, "I am putting into your hands Jericho, with its king and all its brave soldiers. You and your soldiers are to march around the city once a day for six days. Seven priests, each carrying a trumpet, are to go in front of the covenant box. On the seventh day you and your soldiers are to march around the city seven times while the priests blow the trumpets. The seventh time around, when the priests were about to sound the trumpets, Joshua ordered the people to shout, and he said, "the lord has given you the city! So, the priests blew the trumpets. As soon as the people heard it, they gave a loud shout, and the walls collapsed. Then all the army went straight up the hill into the city and captured it.

*   *The gates of Jericho were kept shut and guarded to keep the Israelites out. No one could enter or leave the city. The lord said to Joshua, "I am putting into your hands Jericho, with its king and all its brave soldiers.*

•   *In Joshua 6:1 - 2 - A whole city shut their gates   no influx of business allowed, because they were trying to hinder some people.*

16.   Lord, in spite of every attempt to restrict my access to my allocated territory, today, I cause a panic in the camp of they who have caused me delay.

•   *Every wall built by humans has a weak point   I wonder if the reason the walls of Jericho crumbled from the shouting was because it had originally failed the vibration test!!!! Everyone has a price, .when you present their price, they budge.*

17. Lord, as I obey you, please show me the weak points in the laws that they have used to restrict me from gainful access.

- *When you are acting in obedience, but no result is obvious, yet again, you become weary and struggle to go on.*

18. Lord, give me the resilience to carry out dutifully the instructions that will lead to my access.

Deuteronomy 11:22 - 25 (NCV)

If you are careful to obey every command I am giving you to follow, and love the lord your god, and do what he has told you to do, and are loyal to him, then the Lord will force all those nations out of the land ahead of you, and you will take the land from nations that are bigger and stronger than you. Everywhere you step will be yours. No one will be able to stop you. The lord your God will do what he promised and will make the people afraid everywhere you go.

19. Lord, in this season, month and year, for me to have easy access, force nations out of the land ahead of me.

- *When you need to take the land from nations that are bigger and stronger than you, you better have something they don't have and know something they don't know.*

20. Lord, I receive supernatural wisdom to invade the decision-making platforms within my desired territories.

- *Some of you know that where you are is far from where you were meant to be...but only one person's decision has put your life on hold for this long.*

21. According to the word of the lord, I decree, no one will be able to stop me from accessing the lands allocated to me.

- *No man*
- *No woman*
- *No adult*
- *No child*
- *No kingdom*

- *No land*

- *No authority*

- *After praying, Esther appeared, what would have killed other people was waived for her   the king did not call, she went in because she had a need.*

22. Lord, even when I do not conform to pre-existing arrangements and norms, in this season, month and year, whatever effort I put in to access my great place will be met with rewarding acknowledgement.

- *In Matthew 16:17,19 - I will give you the keys to the kingdom.Secrets are locked in safes. To open a safe, you need the code. When you have the code, whatever treasures in there, you will have access to.*

23. From the scripture above, revelation led to receiving keys. Through out this season, month and year, I will be given the codes I need to access locked away treasures.

- *Access to answers*

Matthew 16:13-19 (MSG)

And that's not all. You will have complete and free

access to god's kingdom, keys to open any and every door: No more barriers between heaven and earth, earth and heaven. A yes on earth is yes in heaven. A no on earth is no in heaven."

24. From this season, month and year, every prayer I make be in line with the word of God and will receive speedy answers.

- *Many shout, beat themselves, fight others, and still get no answers.*

25. I receive keys to open any and every door that God has designed for me   I receive the code to access great secrets of the earth. I receive codes to access treasures that will last for me

26. From this season, month and onwards, I receive ease of access to a life of unrestrained pleasing results.

Access to help

- *Ease of access for they that will help me.*

Daniel 10:12 - 14 (CEB)

Then the man said to me, "Don't be afraid, Daniel, because from the day you first set your mind to understand things and to humble yourself before your god, your words were heard. I've come because of your words! For twenty-one days, the leader of the Persian kingdom blocked my way. But then Michael, one of the highest leaders, came to help me. I left Joshua there with the leader of the Persian kingdom. But I've come to help you understand what will happen to your people in the future.

- *In the UK, when you hear the sound of a siren, it means all should stay clear of the access route. If you block the access for an ambulance or fire truck transporting a person in need and they die, you could be charged for murder or related crimes. The worst thing that can happen to a man is for your helper to be made handicapped.*

27. In this season, month and year, the help that is allocated to me will have ease of access to reach me.

28. Lord I decree that in this season, month and year, they that will help me will have ease of access to what they require to help me. Every person who was supposed to help me but has become delayed as well, I decree that the path clears for them this season, month and year in

Jesus name.

- *Lift up your heads oh ye gates and be ye lifted the everlasting doors! I receive ease of access in this season.*

I decree increase by heavenly mandate according to the words of your prayer and in line with the word of God, that ease shall locate you wherever you are in the name of Jesus.

120   POSSESSING THE GATE

CHAPTER 10:
EASE OF SUPERNATURAL HELP

Let me start by sharing a story with you. A friend of mine used to visit a shop to buy groceries and was always served by the same gentleman. One day as she knelt to pray, she found out that she could not stop thinking about this man.

She just could not proceed. After a while, she got up and concluded the prayer session. A few days later, the same thing happened. She went to the grocery store to ask after the man. While talking with him, she discovered that he was an immigrant and he had his wife and children in another country, who were also in desperate need of help. She intervened and offered them assistance..

Being human, even I will take care of my needs before considering helping others. Today, we will pray for your destiny helpers.

Isaiah 25:6 (CEV)

On this mountain the lord all-powerful will prepare for all nations a feast of the finest foods. Choice wines and the best meats will be served.

1   I decree that God will authorize a feast of fat things for

you my destiny helper

2   Your help will be delivered to you promptly.

3   Favour begets favour, my helpers of destiny, from today, you will experience favour that can only be tagged humanly ridiculous and impossible.

4   As you experience ease and help in your own lives, your minds will be at peace.

Daniel 10:12-13 (AMP)

> *Then he said to me, "do not be afraid, Daniel, for from the first day that you set your heart on understanding this and on humbling yourself before your god, your words were heard, and i have come in response to your words. But the prince of the kingdom of Persia was standing in opposition to me for twenty-one days. Then, behold, Michael, one of the Chief [of the celestial] princes, came to help me, for i had been left there with the kings of Persia.*

> ** A while ago, I saw a documentary about a man who was struggling through life and for him, times were hard. He prayed for a long time, but there was no change.*

One day, the lord showed him a vision. He saw that his prospective helpers were tied up, and this had hindered everyone who was scheduled to help him.. As soon as anyone decided to assist him, they would also become caught up with personal life challenges. Until the lord opened his eyes and he prayed the right prayers, this man continued to struggle.

3. Every life challenge that you will face, which will syphon and waste the seeds you are meant to sow into my life, I decree that the God of heaven will save you from them beforehand.

4. My helpers, you will not give up on helping me due to difficulties.

5. The lord shall lead you promptly into great resources.

6. They that are meant to give you that which you need to give me will not hold back.

7. As you experience plenty, the Lord, will keep mentioning me to you.

8. As you mention me to them Lord, they will not argue or delay.

9. Because I am a fertile ground, they will see a positive change that helping me will bring to their lives.

10. Lord, every blessing that you will give me this season, month and year, is in the hands of someone now, promptly cause them to release them to me.

I decree increase by heavenly mandate according to the words of your prayer and in line with the word of God, that ease shall locate you wherever you are in the name of Jesus.

Galatians 5:22
Fruit of the Spirit
Love
Joy
peace
Long suffering
Kindness
goodness
faithfulness
gentleness
self control

v.24 And those who are Christ's have Crucified the flesh with its passions and desires.
If we live in the Spirit, let us also walk in the Spirit.

26. Let us not become conceited, provoking one another, envying one another.

Printed in Great Britain
by Amazon